The Making of a Champion

A World-Class Mountain Biker

Heinemann Library

Chicago, Illinois

Paul Mason

© 2004 Heinemann Library
a division of Reed Elsevier Inc.
Chicago, Illinois

Customer Service 888-454-2279

Visit our website at www.heinemannlibrary.com

Designed by Heinemann Library
Printed in China by WKT Company Limited.

08 07 06 05 04
10 9 8 7 6 5 4 3 2 1

Library of Congress Cataloging-in-Publication Data

Mason, Paul, 1967-
  A world-class mountain biker / Paul Mason.
     p. cm. -- (The making of a champion)
  Includes bibliographical references and index.
  ISBN 1-4034-4674-1 (hc-library binding) -- ISBN 1-4034-5536-8 (pb)
  1. All terrain cycling--Juvenile literature. 2. Cyclists--Juvenile literature. I. Title. II. Series.
  GV1056.M36 2004
  796.63--dc22
                                2004000578

Acknowledgments
The publishers would like to thank the following for permission to reproduce photographs:

p. 7 bottom Eric Risberg/AP Photo; p. 30 Geoff Waugh/Buzz; p. 11 top Duomo/Corbis, p. 29 Gabe Palmer/Corbis, p. 35 top Ales Fevzer/Corbis, p. 41 bottom AFP/Corbis; p. 38 Mark Dawson/Fat Tire Foto; p. 14 insets Paul Mason; p. 41 top EPA/PA Photos; p. 4 Mark Dawson/Stockfile, p. 5, p. 6 Steven Behr/Stockfile, p. 7 top, p. 8 Seb Rogers/Stockfile, p. 9 Steven Behr/Stockfile, p.10, p. 11 bottom, p. 12, p. 14 left, p. 14 right, p. 16, p. 18, p. 19, p. 20, p. 21 top, p. 21 bottom Dave Stewart/Stockfile, p. 22 Steven Behr/Stockfile, p. 23 top, p. 23 bottom, p. 24, p. 25, p. 26, p. 27 top, p. 27 bottom, p. 28, p. 31, p. 32, p. 33 right, p. 33 left, p. 34, p. 35 bottom, p. 36, p. 37, p. 39 top, p. 39 bottom Mark Dawson/Stockfile, p. 40 Steven Behr/Stockfile, p. 42, p. 43 top, p. 43 bottom; p. 13 x 3, p. 15 Trek Bicycle Corporation.

Cover photograph reproduced with permission of Stockfile/Steven Behr.

Every effort has been made to contact copyright holders of any material reproduced in this book. Any omissions will be rectified in subsequent printings if notice is given to the publishers.

Contents

Battle with gravity

One of the most exciting mountain bike events is the downhill. As with ski racing, the riders go one after another down a preset course. The winner is whomever gets to the bottom in the quickest time. The 2003 women's World Championship downhill event saw a classic battle between the most successful racer ever, France's Anne-Caroline Chausson, and the world's other top racers.

Hot competition

Anne-Caroline Chausson was the racer all the other riders feared most and the favorite to win. She was world BMX champion in 1993, world downhill junior champion from 1993 to 1995, and world champion for six years from 1996 to 2002. Victory would bring "Anne-Caro" yet another world downhill championship to add to her collection of titles.

However, some of the world's best riders were also in the field, desperate to end Chausson's winning run. Great Britain's Fionn Griffiths and Tracey Moseley, second and third in the 2002 championships, were there. So, too, were Kathy Pruitt and Marla Streb of the United States and Sabrina Jonnier and Nolvenn Le Caer of France, Chausson's teammates. The stage was set for one of the most thrilling downhill races in years.

Marla Streb races in full body armor on the World Cup downhill course at Lugano, Switzerland, in 2003. Competitors found the steep, rocky course demanding.

The course

The competition at Lugano was held over a steep, technically challenging 1.2-mile (1-kilometer) course. As 2003 U.S. champion Marla Streb said, "Most people made mistakes on the course because of their hands and arms being so tired... those that had the most relaxed hands throughout the run [were] able to ride the bottom of the course clean." The rider who used least amount of energy on the demanding upper part of the course was probably going to win.

Many riders struggled with the challenges posed by the tricky route, in which they needed to use a combination of skill and strength to get through the tight turns and rocky sections. But late in the competition, Britain's Tracey Moseley posted a fast time of 5:33.31. With only eight riders to go, Moseley was in the lead and looking like she would win a medal.

But then came the French women's team assault on the course. First, Nolvenn Le Caer posted a faster time, and then Sabrina Jonnier pushed Moseley into third. Finally, Chausson launched herself down the course. Riding at a different level from the others, she sliced huge chunks of time from her competitors. Her final time of 5:10.23 was 12 seconds faster than silver medalist Jonnier.

Anne-Caroline Chausson

Nickname:	Anne-Caro
Born:	1977
Country:	France
Height:	5'6" (172 cm)
Weight:	130 lbs (59 kg)
Hobbies:	Skiing, traveling
Favorite food:	Seafood
Dislikes:	Soccer, chocolate cake, snakes, people too proud of themselves

Chausson is the most successful mountain biker ever. By the age of 23, she had won more World Cup races in a single discipline (downhill) than any other rider.

What is mountain biking?

Mountain biking first started in California during the 1970s. Friends would get together and race beach cruisers downhill. When they reached the bottom, they would throw them in the back of a pickup truck, drive back up the hill, and do it again. Mountain biking has since become an Olympic sport.

Cross-country

Cross-country racing is the type of mountain biking that has been featured in the Olympics since 1996. The riders compete over a circular course, riding lightweight bikes. Cross-country courses differ from place to place. Some courses are relatively flat and smooth, which suits riders who are good at riding at a constant high speed. Other courses are bumpier and have more hills. These courses suit riders who enjoy varying their speed and can deal with difficult obstacles.

Dual slalom and 4x

In dual slalom competitions, two riders at a time race down a course side-by-side, through specially built jumps and turns. The winner goes through to the next round, and the racing continues until one rider is crowned champion. Recently, a similar type of racing called 4x has become popular. It features four riders instead of two.

Women's racing is every bit as tough as the men's competitions—as this shot of a 4x race shows!

Downhill

In downhill racing, the riders race one after another down a seemingly impossible route. They perform jumps and slides as they look for the fastest way down the course. Full-face helmets and body armor are crucial, as crashes can be very dangerous. The rider who gets down the hill fastest wins.

Endurance racing

Over the last few years, the number of endurance races has increased dramatically. In these, teams of riders race over a set time period, usually 24 hours. They ride one at a time, as a relay team. The challenge is to go further in 24 hours than any other team.

Endurance events test riders and their equipment to the limit. Often there are mechanics and massage therapists to fix to damaged bikes and help aching riders.

Thomas Frischknecht

Nickname:	Frischi
Born:	1970
Country:	Switzerland
Height:	5'8" (176 cm)
Weight:	148 lbs (67 kg)
Favorite rock group:	U2
Favorite food:	Sushi

Frischi is a legendary rider. He was a world junior **cyclo-cross** champion and also races on the road. By the end of 2003, he had won nine mountain biking World Championships, seventeen World Cup race victories, a European Championship, a silver medal in the 1996 Olympics in Atlanta, Georgia. He also finished in sixth place in the 2000 Olympics in Sydney.

Getting started

It can be easy to get carried away with the expensive bikes and equipment that are available for mountain biking. But most top riders started their careers on inexpensive, simple bikes and only moved on to expensive gear later. The first mountain bikers, after all, rode very simple bikes, which are not even what we think of as mountain bikes today.

Matching the terrain

Top riders choose different bikes for different competitions. However, most people have one bike for every kind of ride. Generally, most bikes with knobby tires (tires that have shaped knobs on them, rather than being smooth) and a wide range of gears can be used off-road.

It is important, though, that your bike is always strong enough for the job you want it to do. Jumps or extreme downhill routes on a lightweight cross-country bike can result in the bike breaking or the rider suffering injury.

Basic requirements

The basic equipment of mountain bikers are simple. They need a bike that will go off-road, a helmet, some water, suitable clothes (warm if the weather is cold, cool if the weather is hot), a pump and puncture repair kit, and a clear idea of where to go.

Not everyone rides in the snow. But varying weather and landscapes are one of the attractions of mountain biking.

First ride

Most people first get into mountain biking when a friend persuades him or her to come along on a ride. Often this first ride turns out to be surprisingly hard work. People who have only ridden a bike on the road generally find off-road riding a lot tougher than they expect. The bike slips and slides, and the rough ground makes it hard to keep an even pedaling speed.

What usually persuades people to try mountain biking again is the speed and excitement of the sport. Racing your friends up a hill and then speeding down the other side, hanging on to the brakes to slow down, can be very exciting.

Ride planning

It is important that everyone on a ride knows where she or he is going and how to get back. Experienced bikers often build in an "escape route"—a way of shortening the ride if it is taking too long or someone gets too tired to finish the full route. It is also important to learn how to repair a puncture, as these can be common.

Puncture facts

- Special mountain-bike tires and inner tubes are available that are more puncture-resistant than regular inner tubes.
- Some racers carry gas canisters that allow them to reinflate their tires quickly.

One thing all mountain bikers get to learn sooner or later is how to fix a puncture. All riders should practice this skill. Having to fix a puncture for the first time in a race would be disastrous.

Starting to race

Racers such as Sue Thomas, the top British cross-country rider in 2003, or Nathan Rennie of Australia, the 2003 World Cup downhill winner, were not always at the top of their sport. They once were just normal kids who were interested in cycling. So, how did they end up as leading members of their national mountain-bike teams?

Early races

People get into mountain-bike racing in many ways. Some start by entering a race for fun. Others might come from a BMX, road racing, or even motorcycle background. Wherever they come from, a few people finish their first race and immediately decide never to do another one! But many love the competition and become determined to do better next time. This is usually when they consider joining a club.

Joining a club

Riders can find out about a club near them through USA Cycling. USA Cycling is the official U.S. cycling organization. Joining a mountain-bike club has several advantages for newcomers. Most importantly, they get access to a qualified cycling coach. Coaches will be able to give advice on training and help riders with their technique and race tactics.

If a racer starts to do very well in competitions—perhaps finishing in the top three in most events—he or she might be asked to represent the region in national competitions. If he or she continues to win, the biker may even get to join the national team. At this level, racers usually get support from the national organization. This usually means help with training and coaching and probably some financial support.

Coaches play a big part in the careers of most top riders. Great Britain's Sue Thomas, shown here racing in 2003, was once asked who had most influenced her riding. She replied, "My old coach—I worked with Martin Early for about four years... he's been a [huge] influence."

Developing cyclists

One of the main duties of USA Cycling is to find, train, and select cyclists to represent the United States in international competitions. So, once a young rider begins to have success at the local level, he or she might be able to attend one of USA Cycling's regional development camps. At these camps, promising young cyclists are exposed to excellent coaching and top competitors from all over the country.

Riders like this gain valuable experience in racing by starting young.

Roland Green

Born: 1974
Country: Canada
Height: 5'9" (180 cm)
Weight: 161 lbs (73 kg)
Honors: Cross-country 2001 and 2002 World Champion; 2001 World Cup series winner and National Off-Road Bicycle Association (NORBA) winner.

Green's cycling career started because he wanted a few extra minutes in bed before school! He would let the school bus go then race after it on his bike. Throughout his career, he has had to overcome the challenge of a serious allergy to pollen. This made racing in the spring and early summer extremely difficult.

Roland Green goes through race preparations. The earpiece will keep him in contact with his coach, who gives advice on race tactics.

Parts of a bike

The bikes used by top riders, such as 2001 world champion Alison Dunlap, are complex pieces of engineering wizardry. Unbelievably light, they weigh as little 19 pounds (8.5 kilograms) and cost thousands of dollars. The advanced technology that goes into these bikes—at least some of it—goes into most models that a manufacturer makes. Even a manufacturer's least expensive mountain bikes are fine for off-road riding and racing.

Frames

The frame is the heart of every mountain bike. It has to be stiff enough not to bend as the rider puts pressure on the pedals and light enough to make pedaling easy. Cross-country frames do not need to be as strong as downhill or dual slalom frames. For this reason, cross-country frames are often thinner to reduce weight.

Wheels and tires

As well as light frames, cross-country racers use wheels with lightweight rims and tires and a reduced number of spokes. Downhill racers have gravity on their side helping them speed downhill, so they rarely worry about wheel weight. For them, it is important that the wheel is strong enough to not break or become damaged.

Position facts

Cross-country bikes usually have the saddle at about the same height as the handlebars, to give a more aerodynamic, powerful pedaling position. Downhill bikes have the saddle set much lower. The rider does not need to pedal much but will need to keep his or her weight further back to avoid being thrown over the handlebars.

Christopher Kovarik of Australia is pictured here on a typical downhill bike. He has shifted his weight way back to balance the bike on the steep downhill slope. Otherwise, he would risk going over the handlebars.

Handlebars

Cross-country bikes use flat or nearly flat handlebars, to help the rider keep an aerodynamic position. Downhill bikes tend to have wider, higher bars to give the rider a more upright riding position. That way the rider can more easily see the obstacles that lie ahead.

Groupset

"Groupset" is the name given to all the other components that make up a bike—the brakes, gears, and chain, for example. Some groupsets are lighter than others, but most groupsets made by big manufacturers tend to work well.

saddle

triple chainset with three rings on the front

V-brakes work by holding a rubber pad on the wheel rim.

seat tube

top tube

down tube

head tube

rear brakes

eight-, nine-, or ten-speed rear derailleur

A clipless pedal attaches to a cleat on the bottom of a rider's shoe.

Cross-country riders usually just have front suspension, to absorb the worst vibrations from the trail.

This is a typical cross-country bike. Although some bikes are more expensive than others, all share the same basic features.

Biking equipment

Mountain bike racers have to be ready to train and compete in all kinds of weather and conditions. The 2004 Athens Olympics took place in the searing heat of a Greek summer, and the gold-medal winners there did their Olympic training in similar conditions. But races are held around the world—from the tropical heat of Cairns in Australia to the chilly air of the Swiss Alps in springtime—so it is always important to be prepared.

Summer-biking gear

Essential summer biking gear includes:
- Lycra shorts with padded insert to improve comfort.
- A cycling jersey with a long zipper for ventilation.
- Shoes with mesh tops for ventilation.
- Lightweight, fingerless gloves to improve comfort for hands.

Winter-biking gear

Essential winter biking gear includes:
- Thermal tights worn over shorts, or alone if padded
- Thermal base layer
- Fleece
- Jacket with a windproof front to stay warm
- Winter shoes with neoprene cuffs to keep out water and mud
- Padded, windproof fleece gloves to keep fingers warm.

Clothing

Most riders avoid wearing loose clothing on a bike. Clothes that are close-fitting are best, because they offer less wind resistance and are unlikely to get caught in a bike's moving parts.

Tools

Most riders carry a small tool kit with them. At a minimum, racers would normally carry:

- a tool with a selection of allen keys (l-shaped tools for tightening and loosening bolts), a small flat-head screwdriver, and one or two spanners (wrenches)
- a chain splitter (a device that allows them to repair a broken chain)
- a puncture-repair kit
- a bicycle pump to reinflate tires.

Hydration

It is important that world-class athletes drink plenty of water during a race. A sports drink will also help replace the salts and other nutrients they lose. Most riders carry their drink in a water bottle held in a cage on the bike frame. Others prefer to wear a backpack with a special water container. This allows the rider to suck his or her drink through a tube from the pack while the race is in progress, without taking her or his hands off the handlebars. The packs can also be used to carry tools and spare clothes.

All serious mountain bikers should have a small tool like this one.

Safety gear

All racers are required to wear a helmet whenever they ride on a mountain bike. In the past, helmets were uncomfortable and sweaty, but today they are light and have great ventilation.

Downhill racers take protection even more seriously than cross-country riders. This is probably no surprise, considering that they travel downhill at speeds of more than 40 miles per hour. (60 kilometers per hour). Downhillers wear full-face helmets and body armor to protect themselves if they crash.

Adjusting the bike

A mountain bike has to correctly fit the rider in order for him or her to ride it as fast as possible. Professional racers, such as Filip Meirhaeghe of Belgium, usually have their bikes specially made, with the frame providing an exact fit to the lengths of their legs, body, and arms. But any bike can usually be adjusted to give the rider a little extra speed.

Biomechanical efficiency

The goal when setting up a bike is to allow the rider to squeeze the maximum efficiency possible from his or her pedaling. A rider's position on the bike needs to mix aerodynamic shape with comfort. If a rider is too hunched over, she or he will not be able to breathe right or to see obstacles on the route. If the rider is too upright, he or she will be held back by extra wind resistance.

Filip Meirhaeghe, one of the world's top mountain-bike racers, sprints across the finish line at the end of one of the 2003 World Cup cross-country races.

Frame fact

On a mountain bike, the frame has a sloping top tube to avoid accidents in which the rider gets injured on the top tube. Most riders aim to have about a 3–4-inch (80–100-millimeters) gap between the top tube and themselves while standing on the floor.

Saddle height and position

Many riders first set their saddle height by sitting on the bike in their bike shoes, with one heel on a pedal. The saddle is the right height if the rider's knee is slightly bent when the pedal is at the bottom of its revolution (turn). If the rider's hips rock from side to side once he or she starts pedaling, the saddle is set too high and may cause an injury. It must be lowered an inch or two.

Saddle position is set using a plumb line. Riders move the saddle back and forth until a plumb line dangling from just behind the kneecap goes straight through the pedal spindle when the crank is parallel to the ground.

Cleats

Riders using clipless pedals normally set their shoe cleats so that the pedal spindle is under the ball of their foot.

Stem and handlebars

The last adjustment riders make is to the handlebars. Many use a common rule of thumb that says that if the axle of the front wheel is hidden from view behind the handlebars, the "reach" is right. If the axle is behind the bars, a shorter stem may be needed. If the axle is in front, a longer stem would provide a more aerodynamic position.

This diagram shows how to make sure a bike's saddle and handlebars are set at the correct height.

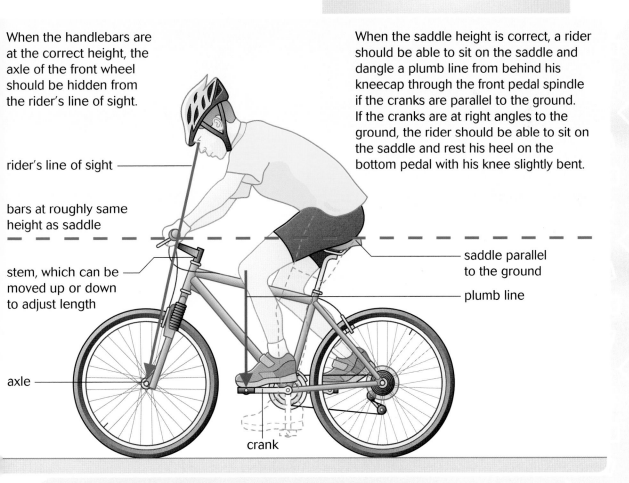

When the handlebars are at the correct height, the axle of the front wheel should be hidden from the rider's line of sight.

When the saddle height is correct, a rider should be able to sit on the saddle and dangle a plumb line from behind his kneecap through the front pedal spindle if the cranks are parallel to the ground. If the cranks are at right angles to the ground, the rider should be able to sit on the saddle and rest his heel on the bottom pedal with his knee slightly bent.

rider's line of sight

bars at roughly same height as saddle

stem, which can be moved up or down to adjust length

saddle parallel to the ground

plumb line

axle

crank

Riding style

Race commentators often mention that a particular rider has his or her own style. Riding style refers to several factors, such as the racer's position on the bike, his or her pedaling action, and how the rider holds his or her head. Most world-class cyclists want to have as smooth a style as possible, channeling all their energy into their pedal power.

Cadence and gears

The speed at which a rider turns the pedals is known as their cadence. The correct cadence is affected by weather conditions. Riding into the wind may require a higher cadence and an easier gear than riding with the wind behind you, for example.

Generally, most riders are comfortable at a cadence of 70 to 80 rpm (revolutions per minute), which is just more than one pedal revolution per second. The most experienced racers may have a higher cadence of 80 to 90 rpm.

Christof Sauser of Switzerland shows solid uphill technique—his elbows are bent and his weight is forward to keep the front wheel from lifting as he drives ahead. He will use a gear on the bike that requires him to push hard but still keep the pedals spinning. Once the pedal strokes become too slow, it is very easy to lose speed.

Climbing hills

Inexperienced mountain-bike riders often try to ride uphill staying in the same gear and end up having to stand up on the pedals, rocking the bike from side to side and using their upper body to add power. Over a long climb this is exhausting. Standing up like this also takes weight off the back wheel, making it more likely to slip on any loose ground.

Top racers such as Mary Grigson, a five-time Australian national champion (1998–2002), select an easier gear to ride uphill. This allows them to keep a higher cadence, which has two main advantages. First, they can stay in the saddle, which drains much less energy than standing up on the pedals. Second, a higher cadence allows them to ride up sudden increases in the slope much more easily.

Shifting fact

Top cross-country racers want to keep their cadence steady on hills. They do this by shifting gears early, before their cadence starts to drop.

Gunn-Rita Dahle

Born: 1973
Country: Norway
Height: 5'7" (173 cm)
Weight: 141 lbs (64 kg)
Hobbies: Kittens, hiking, and reading

Dahle was world and European cross-country champion in 2002 and has been one of the best bikers around since 1996. She has won many World Cup races and is also a good road racer. In 1998 she won one of the stages in the women's Tour de France, the most prestigious road race in the world.

Technique

Uphill riding technique is one of the keys to successful cross-country riding. Downhill racers, though, develop a different set of skills—skills that help them descend very fast. Of course, downhill riding techniques are used in cross-country, too, but in downhill the bikes are stronger and heavier, the slopes steeper, and the racing more extreme.

Taking a line

Expert downhillers such as Britain's Steve Peat make sure they know every inch of the course before a competition. They pick the best line—the smoothest, fastest way through each turn. Then they focus on where they want to go, relaxing their body and allowing it to automatically steer the bike in the right direction.

One mistake newcomers to the sport often make is to look at the ground in front of their wheel, trying to spot small obstacles like stones. The bike will usually flow over these anyway. Looking down increases the feeling of speed and can cause fear. This can make the rider tense, which will increase the likelihood of a crash.

Obstacle fact

Never look at an obstacle you want to avoid (experts call this hazard fixation) or you are almost certain to hit it! Instead, look where you want to go, and the bike should follow.

Great Britain's Steve Peat, world downhill champion in 2002, picks his line through a rocky course in Orgiva, Spain. He lets the front wheel lift away from the rock and keeps his weight back, trusting the bike's suspension to handle the landing.

Grip through turns

Top riders use two techniques to get the maximum tire grip through turns.

First, they look "through" the turn, at the point where the two sides of the trail come together. This is known as the vanishing point. Racers use the vanishing point to judge their speed. If it is coming towards them, the turn is getting tighter and they slow down. If the vanishing point is getting further away, the turn is straightening and they accelerate.

Second, racers try to keep their weight balanced, with enough pressure on the front tire to allow it to grip. It may be okay if the back wheel slides, but if the front wheel slips, a crash is likely.

This rider shows nice downhill technique. His weight is toward the back of the bike, which gives him clear vision ahead and ensures that he does not tip forward over the handlebars. His knees and elbows are bent to help absorb shocks.

Tinker Juarez

Born:	1961
Country:	United States
Height:	5'7" (173 cm)
Weight:	139 lbs (63 kg)

Californian Tinker Juarez's career highlights include being on the Olympic team in 1996 and 2000; being a three-time national cross-country champion in 1994, 1995, and 1998; and winning a silver medal at the 1994 World Cross-Country Championships. Tinker's trademark dreadlocks make him one of the sport's most recognizable figures.

Mountain-bike muscle

Mountain bikers obviously need to have strength in their legs, and of course they do. But top racers make sure their whole bodies are fit, including the upper body, which they use to steer their bikes over rough ground. Strength and flexibility in their abdomens and lower backs also help racers keep efficient positions on the bike.

Endurance and strength

World-class mountain bikers need to train for two different kinds of fitness—endurance and strength. Endurance, also known as aerobic fitness, is the ability to keep your muscles working efficiently over a long period of time. Mountain bikers taking part in a 2-hour cross-country race, or a 24-hour endurance event find their fitness is pushed to the limit. Mile after mile, they will be trying to balance their speed against the distance they have to travel, making sure their muscles do not use up all their energy before the finish.

These members of a race squad are training together. Once one of them stands up on the pedals and sprints for the top of the hill, they all usually follow. But standing up in this way burns a lot of energy and should be done sparingly.

Often several racers get close to the finish line at the same time. This is where the second type of fitness, strength, comes in. The riders must sprint for the finish line in an attempt to win. The contest is no longer about aerobic fitness. With such a short way to go, it becomes a battle to see whose legs are strong enough to get them across the finish line first.

Training

The best way to get in shape for riding a bike is—to ride a bike. Specific mountain bike training techniques include heart-rate training and keeping a training diary (pages 24–25). Many riders also like to combine biking with other types of fitness activities. This makes the training less boring. This is known as cross-training (pages 26–27).

Strength training fact

Many top riders use weight training as a way of building their strength. Normally they use weight training during the off-season, since, as one top coach says, "strength training and cycling don't mix well when done [together]." Cyclists work on their shoulders and neck, chest, arms, back, and abdominal muscles, because these can help when sprinting on the bike. Racers also work on their leg strength using weights.

Lack of training can lead to the humiliation of having to push your bike uphill!

Top rider Brian Lopes uses weights like these—called free weights. Most riders no longer use free weights. Instead, they use weight machines, which control the movement of the weights and make injuries less likely.

Mountain-bike training

Today, top cyclists in most disciplines take a very scientific view of training. Their bodies are seen almost as machines, and great care is taken to make sure they work as well as possible. To do this, the best riders have to do the right amount and degree of training at the correct time.

Heart-rate training

Most top cyclists use a heart-rate monitor as part of their training. This is a portable device that measures the speed at which the rider's heart is beating. Most racers get their maximum heart rate (MHR) by taking their age away from 220. So the maximum heart rate for a 16-year-old rider would be about 204. If their training routine calls for heavy work to increase power and fitness, cyclists aim for a high heart rate—perhaps 85 percent of their maximum. Then, to help their body recover quickly from this hard work, they keep their heart rate low for the next few rides—perhaps to 60 percent of their maximum.

Keeping a training diary

All coaches encourage racers to keep a training diary to record what they have done in training and compare it to their plans. For instance, a week in which racers are expected to cover 72 miles (120 kilometers), how did they do and was it done at the right heart rate? Over the years, a diary also allows a racer to see the types of training that get her or him the best results.

Barrie Clarke, one of Great Britain's most consistent bike racers, trains hard using a heart-rate monitor. This allows him to see the effect his training will have on his fitness and speed.

Overtraining

One of the worst things any biker can do is to overtrain and not allow the body time to recover from a workout. The effects of this can be serious. For example, when Canadian cyclist Peter Reid increased his training with an extra eight hours of cycling, his performances suffered. Reid failed to finish almost all his races in 2001 and 2002. Things only improved after he took a break and began to include two rest days a week in his training routine.

Building rest periods into training schedules is important, but these do not have to be days without exercise. A ride at 60 percent of MHR actually helps riders recover more quickly than complete rest. It increases blood flow, makes nutrients circulate more quickly, and reduces muscle soreness.

It can be tempting to simply get out and ride as often as possible, especially on a sunny day. But top riders plan their training carefully and use a diary to record exactly what they have done.

Cross training

Many riders try to vary their bike training, choosing to add other activities to their routine. This is a good way of increasing their general fitness. It also makes it less likely that the training will become too boring.

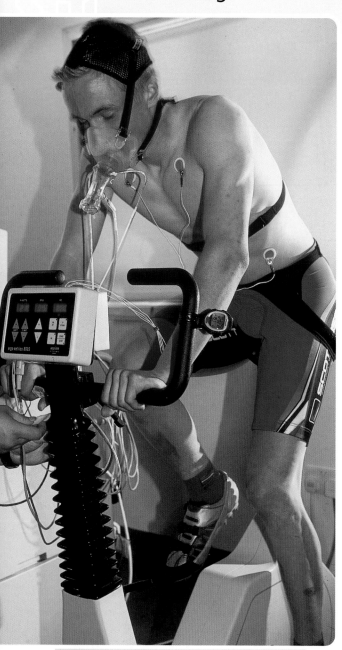

This professional racer looks like a mad scientist's experiment! In fact he is being tested at the Renault Formula 1 Performance Center in Great Britain.

SRM testing

To measure their progress in training, many top riders hook up to a device known as a Schoberer Resistance Measurement (SRM) machine. The machine takes measurements from the bike's cranks and wheels, as well as from monitors worn by the cyclist. These produce a figure measuring the cyclist's power output in watts.

Power-to-weight ratios

Cyclists can use SRM testing to find their ideal racing weight. Dividing a cyclist's power output in watts by their weight in pounds gives a power-to-weight ratio. Cross-country racers aim for as high a power-to-weight ratio as possible.

For example, a cyclist who weighs 143 pounds (65 kilograms) but can put out the same power as one who weighs 165 pounds (70 kilograms) will be able to ride faster. He or she has to move less weight using the same power. But if the rider loses weight, he or she may no longer be able to generate the same power. SRM machines help cyclists tailor their training and food intake to get the best possible power-to-weight ratio.

Heavy training versus racing

During the racing season, most riders maintain their fitness through light workouts. The racing itself pushes their bodies to the limit, so training is geared to keeping aerobic fitness and recovering from the effects of racing. During the off-season, riders put in periods of extremely hard training in order to build their fitness and strength.

Road riding and cyclo-cross

Many mountain bikers use road bikes as part of their training. They can cover more miles than on a mountain bike, getting crucial work for their legs. Riders such Barrie Clarke, one of Great Britain's top mountain-bike racers, also use running, swimming, and cyclo-cross to vary winter training.

Running is good for leg strength and overall fitness, so many top riders use running as a way of varying their training routine.

Great Britain's Jenny Copnall stretches before a race so that her muscles will be relaxed and ready to work. Racing or training with tense muscles can lead to injury.

Stretching and flexibility

Throughout periods of heavy training, it is important for racers to keep muscles flexible. Flexibility describes each muscle's range of movement. Having flexible muscles allows an off-road racer to apply power from unexpected positions— often helpful on a bumpy mountain-bike course.

Cyclo-cross fact

Cyclo-cross is a cross between road racing and mountain biking. Competitions are held on an off-road course using modified road bikes with drop handlebars. Riders often have to carry their bikes over obstacles or up steep slopes.

Healthy eating

Food is a crucial part of any training. On a basic level, if a rider does not eat enough, she or he will "hit the wall"—an expression that means to "run out of energy." But racers also take advice from nutritionists on exactly what they should eat, how much, and when to eat it.

Different food types

Top-level racers, such as the 2000 world champion Marga Fullana of Spain, combine different foods in a very specific way. About 60–65 percent of their calories come from carbohydrates. The body converts carbohydrates into glucose for energy and stores reserve glucose as glycogen.

About 20–25 percent of a top rider's food should be made up of fats, though this would be a high percentage for a normal person. Fat is an important energy source, and as the body runs out of glycogen, it uses fatty acids as an energy source instead. Fat is also a crucial part of nerve fibers and helps regulate the body's temperature.

The last ten to fifteen percent of a racer's diet should be made up of protein, such as lean meat or chicken. Proteins help the body to grow, maintain, and repair itself.

A healthy diet is crucial for riders if they are to train and race well. Otherwise they may "hit the wall"—run out of energy in the middle of a ride.

Carbohydrate fact

There are two different types of carbohydrates, simple and complex. Simple carbohydrates, such as sugar, are absorbed quickly by the body. Complex carbohydrates such as pasta and bread are absorbed more slowly.

Feeding time

Food provides riders with enough energy to go out and train for long hours in the saddle. Most coaches and nutritionists tell riders to eat a good meal before a two- to six-hour training ride. This should include plenty of complex carbohydrates such as bread, pasta, rice, muesli, or oatmeal.

Eating after training is also important. Glycogen is the body's reserve food supply, stored in the liver and muscles. During a tough ride, glycogen gets used up. For the first 30 minutes after exercise, the body opens a "glycogen window," when it is especially able to replace lost glycogen. Eating carbohydrates and some protein while this window is open helps the body to recover more quickly.

Food fact

A top rider can store up to 2,000 calories in their body but will burn 2,500–5,000 on a 4-hour ride. For any ride longer than an hour, riders need to take food with them to eat on the trail, to maintain their energy.

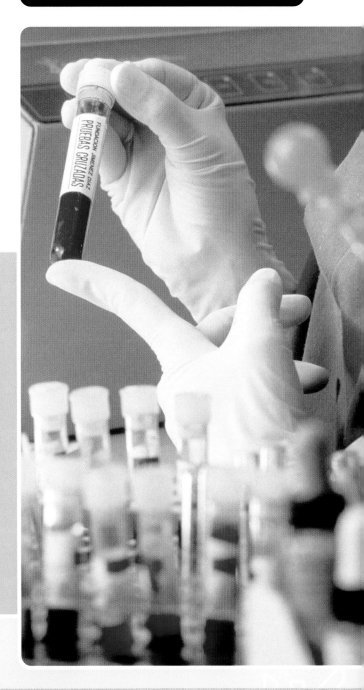

Food supplements and illegal drugs

Many racers take special food supplements to help fuel their bodies. They need to be careful about what is in these supplements, however, as some of them contain illegal performance-enhancing drugs.

For decades, cycling has been associated with illegal drug-taking. A high number of top road-racers have died of heart problems, which are often connected to drug abuse. Partly because of this, mountain bikers are now subjected to strict tests both at competitions and during training.

Racing fuel

On one of the mountain stages of the 2003 Tour de France, race favorite Lance Armstrong suddenly began to struggle. He later explained that he had "hit the wall"—run out of energy—and could have lost the whole race through the simple mistake of not eating enough.

Race lead-in

Racing cyclists once thought the best food they could eat was steak—preferably as raw as possible. Today, nutritionists understand better how food affects a cyclist. While protein-rich foods such as steak are important, today's racers eat a more balanced diet.

Two or three days before a race, most cross-country and mountain-bike riders try to make sure they eat plenty of carbohydrates and drink lots of fluid. Typical meals might include a breakfast of cereal, fruit, or pasta and then a lunch and dinner of bean stew, pasta or rice, potatoes, vegetables, and meat (usually lean red meat or white meat such as chicken).

A quick snack during a long race helps keep competitors' energy levels up. Racers practice eating (and drinking from a water bottle) while riding, so they can do it easily in races.

Race-day food

About three hours before the start of their race, riders eat a "race breakfast"—something rich in carbohydrates, with extra protein—maybe rice or pasta with an egg on top. They avoid anything too sugary, because the simple carbohydrates in sugar would be broken down too quickly to benefit them in the race.

Intake fact

Top riders live by the rule—"Eat before you're hungry and drink before you're thirsty." Taking small amounts of liquid and food regularly helps keep energy levels high.

About 40 minutes before the start of the race, a racer might eat a banana or an energy bar and drink a sports drink. This makes sure they have some fuel in their stomach at race time. In races of less than an hour, no food needs to be eaten during the actual race itself. But during longer races, riders usually start eating a little food every hour after the first hour has passed.

Vegetarian cyclists

Vegetarian racers, such as 2002 world cross-country champion Gunn-Rita Dahle, are careful to take in plenty of iron in their diet. Iron is an essential part of blood, helping carry oxygen to muscles, and it is lost through heavy sweating. Nonvegetarians get their iron from meat. Vegetarian cyclists get iron from nuts, spinach, broccoli, dried fruit, or iron supplements.

Racers get water at a feeding center during a short road-based leg of a mountain-bike race in the European Alps.

Drinks fact

Sports drinks that contain high levels of carbohydrates—needed by cyclists to provide energy—take about ten minutes to work on the body.

Support crew

Behind most successful racers there is a whole team of people helping them to perform as well as possible. National and professional racing teams have mechanics, team managers, coaches, physiotherapists, and sports psychologists to help the riders stay healthy, train better, and ultimately win competitions.

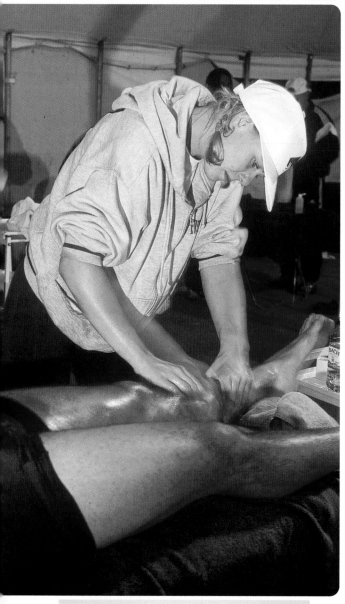

A leg massage after a race or a hard training session can help a rider's muscles recover more quickly than normal. Many top teams have a massage therapist as part of their support crew.

Team support

Coaches and managers of world-class teams are often ex-racers themselves. Gary Foord, for example, is the coach of the British cross-country mountain-biking team. In Foord's previous career as a racer, he won a World Cup event in California and raced in the European Championships and the Olympics. People such as Foord are able to give valuable advice on training, equipment, and race tactics to younger riders.

Physiotherapy and massage

As Foord says, "In training you have to work on the technical side of things, which is physically demanding but also damaging. Potentially you are going to hurt yourself." Many teams have a trained physiotherapist on board to help the racers recover from injuries.

Physiotherapists are experts in how the body works. They explain the best way to keep in shape while suffering from an injury and can give a massage to ease sore muscles. They are most likely to be able to help in cases where injuries have been caused by overtraining or riding in a poor position on the bike.

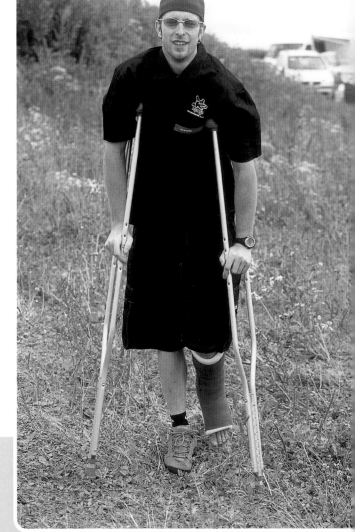

Mechanics are a crucial part of a mountain biker's support team.

Mental training

Increasingly, top athletes of all kinds take advice from sports psychologists. These are experts in the best mental way to approach training and, especially, competition. They tailor their advice to the particular personality of the racer—someone with a naturally aggressive racing style, for example, might need to calm down at the start of a race. Someone who is naturally cautious might get advice that helps them to be more aggressive during races.

Scott Beaumont

Nickname: Boomboom
Born: 1978
Country: Great Britain
Honors: BMX World Champion 1995, 1996; British BMX Champion eight
               times

Beaumont's nickname—Boomboom—is hard-earned, as he has had several serious crashes, including a terrible crash in Telluride, Colorado, in 2002 in which he broke several different leg bones. Despite this, he managed to finish twentieth overall in the World Cup standings.

The biking year

Top riders' lives are geared around the racing season. Athens 2004 Olympic competitors such as Great Britain's Liam Killeen began planning for their races early in 2003. Their training, the events they entered, their vacations—in fact, their whole lives—were focused on those few circuits of the Olympic course. This is because it is crucial for riders to plan and time their training so that they reach their peak for important competitions.

Base conditioning

The mountain-bike racing season usually takes place through the late spring, summer, and early fall. In winter, the riders can put in heavy training, because they are unlikely to have a big race coming up. They work on their base conditioning—the basic strength and fitness that will hopefully allow them to win. Their bodies are pushed to the limit. They may use weights and a variety of other training techniques to get them into good shape for the next season.

Building to a peak

As the racing season begins, the riders start to cut back the intensity of their training. They stop using weights and focus more on the bike techniques and skills that will help them win races. Their workouts on the bike begin to be more concerned with speed and less with distance. This is to prepare their bodies for the rapid acceleration and high pace of racing. It also gives their muscles a chance to recover from the hard work done during the months of tough training.

Liam Killeen has a prerace talk with Dave Brailsford of the British Cycling Federation. The advice of coaches and managers is crucial in helping riders to reach a peak at exactly the right time.

The final countdown

Leading up to a big race such as the World Championships or Olympics, most riders cut down on their training still further. They know they are in shape and in peak form. Their aim now is to get to the starting line in the best condition possible. Light training, with a few sprints, is combined with eating well, drinking lots of fluid, and getting plenty of sleep. The riders want to bring their bodies to peak condition on the day of the race.

This is what a whole year's training often comes down to—crossing the finish line first.

Alison Dunlap

Born: 1969
Country: United States
Height: 5'5" (168 cm)
Weight: 123 lbs (56 kg)
Hobbies: Rock climbing, playing the flute, and skiing

Career highlights:
- UCI Tissot Mountain Bike World Cup Champion 2002
- UCI Mountain Bike World Champion 2001
- Twice Olympic team member: 2000 mountain bike and 1996 road race
- National cross-country champion 1999, 2002

Originally a road racer, Dunlap from Colorado won a stage of the women's Tour de France in 1996, the first by an American since 1989. She turned to pro-mountain biking in 1997. Alison won the NORBA National Championship and UCI World Cup Overall Championship in 2002 while competing with a broken wrist.

Race preparation

All the years of training a rider does can be wasted if he or she fails to get themselves ready on the day of the race. Each rider knows that every little detail has to be checked. All riders need to make last-minute checks. Failing to make them might give the opposition a big advantage.

Rider preparation

Riders, such as the Dutch great Bart Brentjens, time their training schedule to make sure they reach race day in great shape. On the actual day of a race, they ride their bikes to get warmed up and do some stretching to keep relaxed. Several hours before the race they eat a race breakfast. For an event like the cross-country at the 2000 Olympics in Sydney, which lasted a couple of hours during warm weather, they make sure to drink plenty of fluids and have some energy snacks with them.

Equipment preparation

National and professional teams have mechanics to to make sure bikes are running smoothly and are undamaged. As a result, there is less chance of a snapped chain or broken brake cable ruining an important race. Bike mechanics take their work extremely seriously—Lance Armstrong's mechanic on the Tour de France used to sleep with Armstrong's bike next to his bed, just to make sure that no one else was able to touch it!

The mechanic of Great Britain's Steve Peat checks over a bike just ahead of a big race. All top riders have a mechanic to set the bike up and make sure it runs smoothly.

Bike check facts

Most amateur riders have to do their own bike checks before a race. They check that:
- there are no frayed cables that could snap
- brake blocks have plenty of wear on them and are about 3/4 of an inch (2 millimeters) from the rims
- the derailleurs (front and rear) are correctly shifting to all gears
- the saddle and seat post are secure
- the headset, handlebars, and brake levers are secure
- the wheels are tightened, and the quick releases are on.

Coaching and tactics

Before a big race, riders get advice from their coach. This might include suggestions for good times to launch an attack, how to pace the race, and so on. For instance, if a course has a steep uphill section, riders typically keep the pace high along these sections to make sure no one gets ahead of the pack. When they get to the top, the pack relaxes momentarily. A sudden, fierce attack here can allow a rider to take the lead over his or her rivals.

Coaches can also give advice on the technical details of the course— these could include the fastest areas of a long straightaway or the smoothest line through a downhill section.

Roland Green of Canada, the 2002 cross-country world champion, gets some last-minute advice from his coach before the start of a race.

Racing tactics

Even the best plans can go wrong during a race. The riders who can adapt their tactics to changes in the race are usually the ones who come out on top. The story of the women's cross-country race at the 2003 World Championships in Lugano, Switzerland, shows the changes that can affect the outcome of a race.

Leaders emerge

As the riders began to gather at the starting line of the women's cross-country race, the clear favorite was Gunn-Rita Dahle of Norway. Not only was she the current world champion, Dahle had also won every World Cup race that season. But early in the race she suffered a tire puncture, which allowed the other lead riders a chance at victory. By halfway through the six-lap, 23-mile (37-kilometer) course, two riders were ahead of the pack—Alison Sydor of Canada and Margarita Fullana of Spain.

Tactics facts

When two riders find themselves ahead of the others in a race, they have to figure out what they want to do. One rider sometimes decides to ride on the back wheel of the other, effectively getting a "tow" from the rider who leads. Or they can work together, sharing the strain at the front. This gives them a better chance of staying ahead of the rest.

Mountain bikers take off at the start of the 2003 World Championship women's cross-country race.

Working together

Sydor had won three World Championships in a row from 1994 to 1996 and was desperate to win again. She and Fullana decided to ride together for a while. They took turns leading, pushing the pace to try to build up a lead. Then Fullana's bike began to develop mechanical problems, and she fell behind. Then, Sabine Spitz of Germany launched an attack, and she passed Fullana and caught up to Sydor by the end of lap five, with only one lap to go.

Race to the line

Spitz attacked again and opened a small lead. She continued to ride hard. By the time they reached the finish, Spitz had a slight lead. She crossed the finishing line first, with Sydor missing out on a fourth World Championship gold by just sixteen seconds.

Germany's Sabine Spitz races past Alison Sydor on the last lap of the 2003 World Championship women's cross-country.

Spitz celebrates her surprise victory in the 2003 World Championship cross-country race.

Big competitions

Cycling's biggest competitions are those approved by the Union Cycliste Internationale (UCI), or International Cycling Union. The UCI is based in Switzerland and is the world governing body for all kinds of cycling. Road, BMX, mountain biking, and track racing all fall under its control.

Women's downhill racers celebrate on the winner's podium at a round of the World Cup held near Fort William, Scotland.

The World Cup

The World Cup is a series of events held around the world, at which the top riders compete for prize money and World Cup points. The World Cup features downhill and cross-country racing, as well as 4x. At the end of each season, a rider's total points are added up and the winner is crowned. The champion for that year has a good claim to being the world's best rider, as they have performed best over a whole year's racing, rather than in a one event that happens on a single day.

World Championships

Held every year, the "Worlds," as most riders call them, are second only to the Olympics in a mountain-bike racer's mind. The racing includes cross-country, downhill, and 4x. The format is a one-race competition, in which the winner takes all.

Speciality events facts

As well as UCI events, there are special competitions held around the world, usually for TV or video companies to release later. One example of these is the "freeride" events sponsored by a big energy-drink manufacturer. Top downhill riders compete to perform the most spectacular aerials and maneuvers on a preset course or series of jumps.

The Olympics

Since 1996, every four years, the chance has come along to win the biggest prize of all—an Olympic gold medal. But only cross-country riders get the opportunity, as downhill and the other mountain-bike competitions are not Olympic events. For many riders, four years or more of preparation boil down to a couple of hours out on the course.

Alison Dunlap, the 2001 world cross-country champion, has one dream above all others. She says, "My big goal of my cycling career was always to win the Olympics. That's something that I'm focusing on and aiming towards."

Paola Pezzo

Born: 1969
Country: Italy
Height: 5'8" (178 cm)
Weight: 137 lbs (62 kg)
Other sports: Skiing, running

Pezzo is the most successful Olympic mountain biker ever. In Atlanta, Georgia, in 1996 she became the Olympic cross-country mountain bike champion. Then, in Sydney, Australia, in 2000, she beat a world-class field to take a second Olympic gold. Pezzo's favorite color—"Gold!"

Pro rider

The lifestyle of pro riders—professional mountain bikers—can be glamorous. They travel around the world, with other young people who are into the same sport. New bikes are always available, plus other equipment and clothing. Most bikers love their chosen career, but it is not always easy.

Travel

One of the big pluses of being a professional biker is getting the chance to travel. Top riders, such as downhiller Cedric Gracia of Spain, get to visit all the world's top venues, and ride them in small groups or alone. The downside to all this traveling is that pro riders are away from home for long periods without seeing their family and friends. They live out of a suitcase and have to put up with frustrations of international travel—airlines that do not want to take their bikes, delayed flights, and poor accommodations.

Bike development

Many riders are involved in helping develop bikes and other equipment for the companies that employ them. They provide feedback on the geometry (angles and shapes) of the bikes they ride, how they handle, and whether the suspension and brakes work well. Often a bike company's top models are near-direct copies of the machines their racers use. Some racers even have their name attached to a particular model of bike.

"How did this fit in last time?" Packing bikes for travel is a complicated task for international mountain-bike racers.

Working with sponsors

Nonbike companies sometimes sponsor mountain bikers. For example, a car company that makes off-road vehicles might want to be associated with a world champion off-road rider. The riders are given payments or goods—for example, a car—in return for doing publicity work. However, arranging sponsors and financial support can be a tricky job even for top riders. This is especially true in cross-country, which is less appealing to TV audiences than downhill and 4x, and is increasingly difficult to attract sponsors.

Job satisfaction

Despite the difficulties involved, most pro mountain bikers love their work. The covet the excitement and adventure of their lifestyle. And there is always the chance that one day they may become a champion!

Eric Carter clatters his way down the course of one of the 2003 World Cup downhill competitions. It takes years of hard training to become a world-class mountain biker.

Brian Lopes

Country:	United States
Height:	5'7" (175 cm)
Weight:	159 lbs (72 kg)
Hobbies:	Dirtbike riding, weight training, snorkeling, basketball, music
Career highlights:	1998: World Championships Dual Slalom Champion; NORBA National Downhill Champion
	1999: NORBA National Dual Slalom Champion
	2000: UCI World Cup Dual Champion—won seven out of eight UCI World Cup Dual races

A pro BMX rider for eleven years and a pro-mountain biker for nine years, the Californian Brian Lopes is one of the most successful U.S. racers ever.

Mountain-bike champions

Top mountain bikers face tough competition for medals and championships. Even making the top ten in a race requires a biker to be in great shape and an excellent rider. So when you see names like Filip Meirhaeghe of Belgium or Alison Sydor of Canada appear over and over again, you know they are really world-class performers at the top of their sport!

2003 World Cup

Cross-country, women	
1. Gunn-Rita Dahle (Norway)	1,250 points
2. Sabine Spitz (Germany)	875 points
3. Irina Kalentiva (Russia)	715 points

Cross-country, men	
1. Julien Absalon (France)	930 points
2. Christoph Sauser (Switzerland)	845 points
3. Filip Meirhaeghe (Belgium)	693 points

Downhill, women	
1. Sabrina Jonnier (France)	834 points
2. Fionn Griffiths (Great Britain)	814 points
3. Tracy Moseley (Great Britain)	770 points

Downhill, men	
1. Nathan Rennie (Australia)	701 points
2. Cedric Gracia (France)	661 points
3. Mickael Pascal (France)	656 points

2003 World Champions, Lugano, Switzerland

Women's Downhill
1. Anne-Caroline Chausson (France)
2. Sabrina Jonnier (France)
3. Nolvenn Le Caer (France)

Women's Cross-country
1. Sabine Spitz (Germany)
2. Alison Sydor (Canada)
3. Irina Kalentieva (Russia)

Men's Downhill
1. Greg Minnaar (South Africa)
2. Mickael Pascal (France)
3. Fabien Barel (France)

Men's Cross-country
1. Filip Meirhaeghe (Belgium)
2. Ryder Hesjedal (Canada)
3. Roel Paulissen (Belgium)

2000 Olympic champions, Sydney, Australia

Women	
1. Paola Pezzo (Italy)	1:49:24.38
2. Barbara Blatter (Switzerland)	1:49:51.42
3. Margarita Fullana (Spain)	1:49:57.39

Men	
1. Miguel Martinez (France)	2:09:02
2. Filip Meirhaeghe (Belgium)	2:10:05
3. Christoph Sauser (Switzerland)	2:11:20

1996 Olympic champions, Atlanta, Georgia

Women	
1. Paola Pezzo (Italy)	1:50:51
2. Alison Sydor (Canada)	1:51:58
3. Susan Demattei (United States)	1:52:36

Men	
1. Bart Jan Brentjens (Netherlands)	2:17:38
2. Thomas Frischknecht (Switzerland)	2:20:14
3. Miguel Martinez (France)	2:20:36

Glossary

4x event in which four riders race down a course side-by-side

aerobic relating to the amount of oxygen used by the body in exercise

aerobic capacity maximum level of exercise at which the body can get enough oxygen to work without using too much oxygen

aerodynamic capable of avoiding wind resistance

axle pin around which a wheel turns

beach cruiser old-fashioned style of bike with wide handlebars and fat tires

body armor protective clothing worn by people who take part in extreme sports

calorie unit of energy supplied by food

chainset the cranks and cogs at the front of a bike's drive train

cleat device for attaching a cycle shoe to a pedal

cogs also called the freewheel, this usually refers to the block of toothed circles of metal at the back of a bike's drive train

crank "arm" between the pedal and the bike

cyclo-cross sport that mixes cross-country cycling with road bicycles

derailleur hinged device next to the rear whee that allows a cyclist to change gears

drive train pedals, cranks, chain, and gears of a bike

freeride riding without boundaries, using tricks and skills to cover difficult ground and obstacles

full-face helmet helmet with a section that comes around the chin to protect it

gravity force that attracts all objects to one another. The earth has a gravity field that pulls people and objects toward it.

hydrated with an adequate amount of water

lactate threshold point at which the body starts to generate lactic acid in its muscles, as a result of going without enough oxygen

motocross motorbike sport in which competitors race across a series of obstacles on a circular track

nutrient part of food that is needed by living things in order for them to stay alive

nutritionist expert who advises people on the best, healthiest foods to eat

off-season period when riders concentrate on training instead of competitions

pace speed at which something is done

plumb line weighted piece of string that dangles straight downward

rim outer part of the wheel to which the spokes are attached. Tires go on to the outside of the rims.

spoke thin metal rod that joins the hub (center) of the wheel to the rim

sponsor someone who gives money or other support to help an activity take place

Resources

Major international and U.S. organizations

USA Cycling
1 Olympic Plaza
Colorado Springs, Colo. 80909
1-719-866-4596

NORBA-National Off-Road Bicycle Association
1 Olympic Plaza
Colorado Springs, Colo. 80909
1-719-866-4581

UCI-International Cycling Union
CH 1860
Aigle, Switzerland

IOC-International Olympic Committee
Château de Vidy
1007 Lausanne, Switzerland

*To find the organization's website, use a search engine and type in the organization's name as a keyword.

Further reading

Glaser, Jason. *Snow Mountain Biking.* Bloomington, Minn.: Capstone Press, 1999.

King, Andy. *Play-By-Play Mountain Biking.* Minneapolis, Minn.: Sagebrush Education Resources, 2001.

Osborne, Ian. *Mountain Biking.* Minneapolis, Minn.: Lerner Publishing Group, 2003.

Rosenberg, Aaron. *Mountain Biking.* New York City: Rosen Publishing Group, 2002.

Zinn, Lennard. *Zinn and the Art of Mountain Bike Maintenance.* Boulder, Colo.: Velo Press, 2001.

Index